Who is this book for?

This book is written for the countless people who feel like they are somehow out of the loop because they are not sure what hashtags are, nor what all the fuss is about!

I had one client approach me the other day and say that her husband, a social media expert, had explained hashtags to her, but she still didn't really understand – and this woman is by no means a slouch when it comes to business or understanding new concepts – she has a very high-level position and has more than one degree, however the hashtag left her, in her words, "feeling like an idiot".

So, this book is for people like her – intelligent people who just simply don't get the whole "hashtag thing"!

What this book is not

This book is not intended to be an in-depth course into hashtags and/or social media. If you are looking for those, there are plenty out there and we also provide several courses and free webinars.

Also, some of the images may appear a little blurry but we decided it was better to include them and give you blurry screen shots than no images at all...

What this book is

This book is a basic introduction to hashtags so that, when you have finished the book and the activities, you will have a good understanding of hashtags, what they are and more importantly, how to use them to achieve your objectives!

Ready to get started?

OK, are you ready to have some fun? *Don't look at me like that! LOL! I know that if I asked you, you'd say that you most likely also don't really get Twitter and that it's basically a blur across the screen to you, yes? – and that you're really only reading this book because you thought you'd try one last thing to not feel as though everyone is laughing and you have no idea what the joke is all about... It's ok, stick with me and we'll have you laughing with them in no time! ...and if you get to the end and you still have questions, feel free to send them through to me at info@leighstjohn.com.*

Spaces for Your Notes...

At the end of each chapter I've included a blank space for your notes.

Use this area to keep note of your thoughts, interesting hashtags you come across... and if you have any questions, jot them down and then feel free to reach out to me through my website www.LeighStJohn.com and I will make sure your question is answered!

One more thing...

The rate of change is phenomenal in the online world so everything you will read here is current as at Jan 2015 ~ but may have already changed by February! LOL! Regardless, all the basic concepts will stay the same – so read on and let's get you started using hashtags!

ISBN-13: 978-1507667163

ISBN-10: 1507667167

If you would like to invite the author to speak at
an event for your organization, please contact
Leigh St John via the website.

Thanks! :-)

Contents

What is a hashtag?

A hashtag is what many of us know as the pound sign (found at shft+3 on most keyboards).

When the pound sign is placed before a specific word or phrase – with no spaces or other characters – that's a hashtag.

It's a quick way of identifying with a particular brand, event, sentiment or any other grouping.

For instance, if you wanted to participate in the social media conversations around Oprah, you might choose to write your post and put #Oprah at the end of it. That's a hashtag.

At this point I can understand if you think they are confusing and/or unnecessary, but they have become an integral part of the way we communicate online and it's important to know how to use them.

Don't worry if you don't get it at first – just keep reading – it will become clearer.

A hashtag can convey a message or meaning, answer a question, be humorous, informative or provocative to list only a few.

Whenever someone adds a hashtag to their post, it becomes searchable by other users, and when a user clicks on the hashtag, they will be brought to a list of all the posts that have used that hashtag – and in real time. I'll explain this in more detail a little later in this book.

The hashtag's impact on modern language has become so significant that the American Dialect Society declared "hashtag" as the Word Of The Year back in 2012.

NOTES:

When did a pound sign become a hashtag?

There really was a first moment when someone essentially said, 'hey, let's use a hashtag as a way of organizing things!'

That someone was Chris Messina and on August 23, 2007 he posted the following:

Chris Messina™
@chrismessina

how do you feel about using # (pound) for groups. As in #barcamp [msg]?

2:25 PM - 23 Aug 2007

181 RETWEETS 354 FAVORITES

Messina wasn't just some random Twitter user who stumbled upon hashtags by accident. A previous Google employee, the same year (2007) he made that now famous "whisper" (as tweets were known then), he co-founded Citizen Agency, one of the first social media consulting companies.

To put these dates into perspective, Twitter was only founded in March of 2006, with the website going live in July of the same year.

The tipping point for Twitter's popularity was the 2007 South by Southwest Interactive (SXSWi) conference when, during the event, Twitter usage rose three-fold - from 20,000 tweets per day to 60,000 tweets per day.

But the first time a hashtag was used in a major way by the public to categorize tweets was in 2007 when Nate Ritter on October 23rd used Twitter to report on the San Diego fire using the hashtag, #sandiegofire.

In 2009, Twitter updated its system to make hashtags clickable, and providing a search feature for all tweets containing the term.

However, the hashtag has evolved into far more than a categorizing system.

Move forward to today (late December, 2014) and according to internetlivestats.com, every **second**, on average, around **6,000 tweets** are tweeted on Twitter, which corresponds to over **350,000 tweets** sent per minute, **500 million tweets** per day and around **200 billion tweets** per year.

NOTES:

How do hashtags work?

Hashtags are used as a way to group together information so that people can easily find the information they are seeking.

Just as the index in a book groups together mentions of a certain word so you can easily find that for which you are searching, hashtags group together mentions of keywords or key phrases.

When you want to find something in a book, you turn to the index.

When you want to find something online, you turn to the search bar.

To find items that have been posted in social media, you search with the pound sign before the word.

In this example I will use Google Plus – by the way, I know a lot of people have heard of G+ but are not sure how to use it.

For this example, let's look at volunteering – you will see I typed in #volunteering in the search bar:

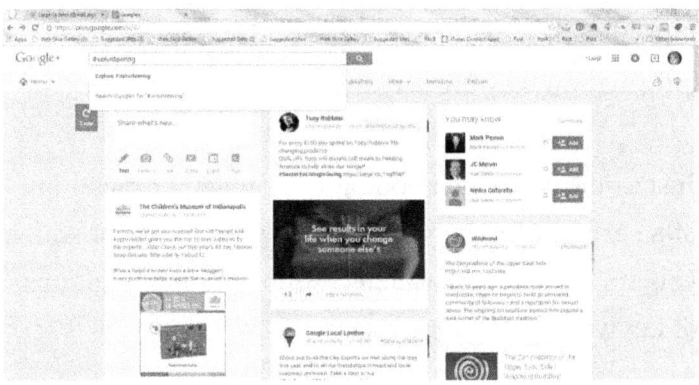

…and this is the result…

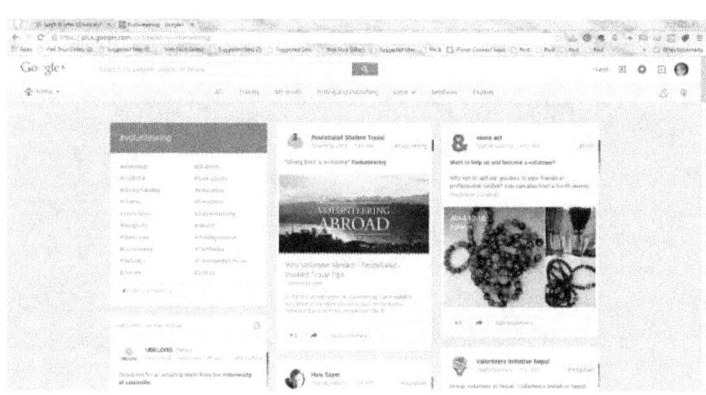

As you can see, my hashtag search not only gave me info on volunteering, it also provided me with a list of other suggested hashtags I might like to try.

NOTES:

Where can I use hashtags – is it only on Twitter?

A lot of people have the misconception that hashtags are only used in Twitter.

The use of hashtags in social media may have started with Twitter, however now hashtags are quite commonplace in almost every social media platform.

Tumblr was one of the early adopters of hashtags when it launched hashtags on August 18, 2009.

Instagram adopted hashtags on January 27, 2011, Flickr added hashtags on March 17, 2013.

It took a while, but Facebook finally incorporated hashtags in June 2013.

Hashtags work on Twitter, Facebook, Pinterest, LinkedIn, Instagram, Google Plus, with more platforms integrating hashtags every day.

So if you aren't using hashtags on these platforms, you are missing out on valuable opportunities to connect with others.

NOTES:

Which Social Media Sites Support Hashtags?

Most social media networks use hashtags in the same basic way; to organize information and make it easier for you, the end user. However, each network has a slightly different approach re how they use them.

Here are just a few of the more common platforms and how to use hashtags within those sites.

Twitter: The site that brought us the hashtag is the most popular social media platform on which to use hashtags.

When you search for a hashtag on Twitter, there are several ways to filter the results to give you what you need.

The "Top" option displays the most relevant and popular posts, including those from users you don't follow.

"All" shows you every tweet that uses the specific hashtag in real time including people you don't follow.

"People you follow" will only display results from users you are following.

Once you have typed in your search term, for example the TV show, #topgear, you will notice on the left that if you click on any of those links, it gives you a list based on the category you clicked.

For instance, if you want photos of #topgear, click on Photos. If you want to see any posts from people near you, click that link.

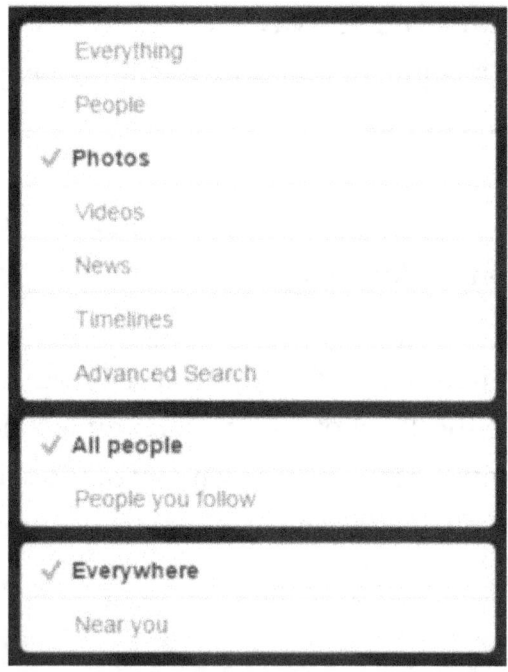

Facebook: Clicking a hashtag on Facebook will bring you to a separate page with posts that include that hashtag. You'll also see the different trending topics in the top right hand corner of your News Feed.

Instagram: Using hashtags on Instagram is a terrific way to see photos similar to the ones that you've taken. Simply hashtag your photo and it will create a link to a page with other pictures of the same subject.

Some hashtags were created specifically for social media community events. #ThrowbackThursday, for example, encourages users to post old photos of themselves.

Google+: Google+ uses hashtags similar to the other sites, but with one main difference. Apart from you adding a hashtag, Google+ will add hashtags to content if they think that it is a relevant and popular keyword.

When you click on a hashtag in Google+, the search results will include the original hashtag as well as posts with similar tags and keywords.

Pinterest: Pinterest uses hashtags, however they're only clickable in a Pin description.

You'll see that as with some other social media sites, Pinterest provides alternatives that are similar or complementary to your hashtag search term:

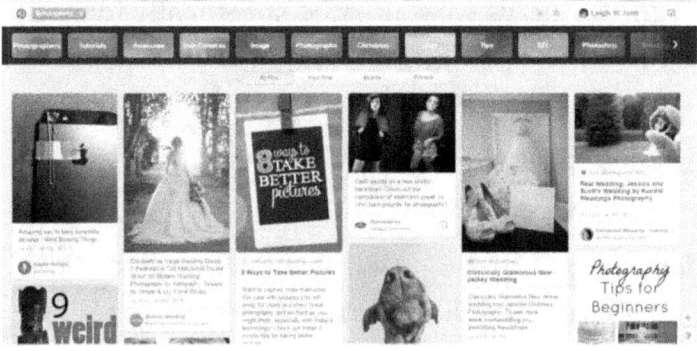

NOTES:

Special note about @ symbol

We won't go into detail here, but keep in mind that the @ symbol does something completely different from the #.

Using the @ symbol in a tweet before a person's Twitter handle (their Twitter username) will tweet at them directly however a # will not.

NOTES:

Why should I use hashtags?

Time is the most valuable asset any of us has.

Quite simply, using hashtags effectively will save you time and make your posting and social media engagement more efficient and enjoyable.

Not only that, but they are an excellent way of promoting your work!

For instance, #amwriting is a hashtag started by Johanna Harness as a way of supporting writers and developing a sense of community.

Here's a tweet that I just made using the #amwriting hashtag:

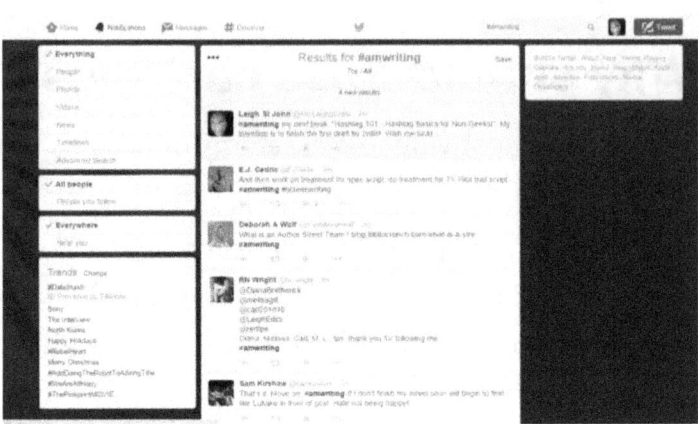

Not only that, but within a few minutes my tweet had been favorited by someone obviously interested in the topic of my book:

This gives me the perfect opportunity to connect with that person and include a link to the website:

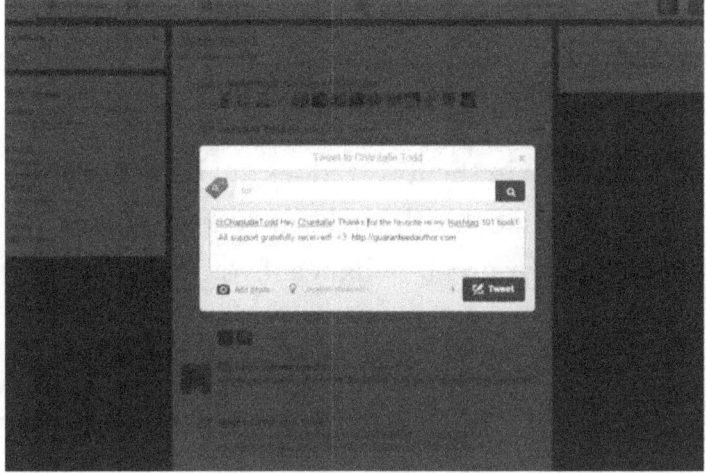

Hashtags are a great way to view in real time events or topics in which you are interested and that are relevant to you. What's more, using hashtags in your posts helps you expand the reach of your tweets and boost your engagement rates.

According to the "Social Media Scientist", **Dan Zarrella**, tweets with one or more hashtags are 55% more likely to be retweeted than tweets without.

So why should you use hashtags?

If a tree falls in the forest, does anybody hear? If you create a post, will anybody read it? There's certainly a far greater chance if you include hashtags.

NOTES:

What characters can I use in a hashtag?

There are limitations on what can be included in a hashtag.

Length

Particularly if you are using Twitter, the length of your hashtag is very important.

Tweets (posts on Twitter) are limited to 140 characters so consider carefully how many of those you are going to use up with your hashtag!

No Special Characters

Hashtags only work with the # sign.

Special characters like "!, $, %, ^, &, *, +, ." will not work. Twitter recognizes the pound sign and then converts the hashtag into a clickable link.

No Spaces

Hashtags do not support spaces. So if you're using two words, skip the space and put the two words together. For example, a hashtag for Richard Branson would be #RichardBranson (and no, capitals don't matter - #richardbranson works just the same).

Be careful with slang

Slang words can have different meanings in different countries and even at different times of the year and in reference to different events, so be very mindful about the words you use. My suggestion is to completely stay away from colloquialisms.

NOTES:

How many hashtags should I use?

If you're thinking the more the better, think again.

Research has shown that anywhere from one to three hashtags in a post is ideal.

The only exceptions to this are for Instagram and Vine where up to seven hashtags have been shown to improve engagement.

NOTES:

How choose which hashtags to use?

First and foremost, your hashtag needs to be relevant to your post.

For instance, even though I am starting to use the hashtag #inspired2achieve as part of my branding, if I created a post about a beautiful flower, that has nothing to do with achievement so that hashtag would be irrelevant.

A good way to discover which hashtags you should use is to look at examples of other people and businesses similar to you. See what they are using and the results.

It's not about playing "follow the follower" but it is a case of making sure that you use hashtags that (a) are relevant to your post and (b) can have a positive effect on the engagement of that post.

When in doubt, it's a good idea to use two hashtags – for instance if your post was about a demonstration at your local Whole Foods store, you would use one for the brand (eg #wholefoods) and one for the community (eg #healthyliving).

Another way of deciding which hashtag to use is to get help from a platform called www.RiteTag.com.

Well-chosen hashtags greatly **increase discovery** by searchers, tag-trackers and hashtag clickers and RiteTag identifies hashtags according to whether they are overused, good, great, or simply not yet used enough to track.

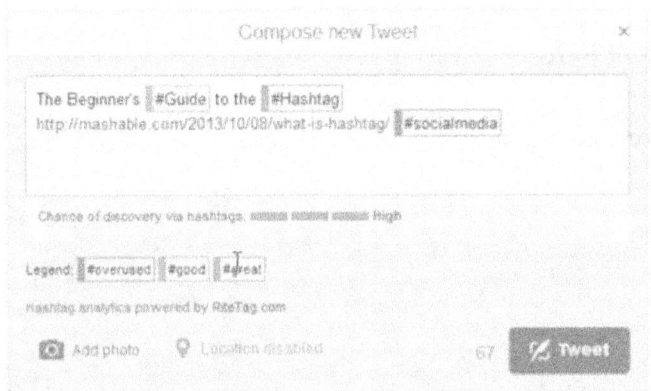

I won't go in to detail about RiteTag here but they have a good video on their home page that explains more.

NOTES:

Where do I use hashtags in a post or tweet?

Hashtags can be used at the beginning, middle or end of a Tweet.

They can also be part of the sentence, such as "It's a #greatday to be alive".

Wherever you use your hashtags, make sure you put them in context. A post that contains only hashtags is confusing and is often viewed as spam.

For instance, if you are a fan of the TV show, 'Breaking Bad', don't post, "#breakingbad #awesome". Put your hashtags into context, eg "I watched the last episode of #breakingbad last night. It was #awesome".

NOTES:

Be careful when you use hashtags

Whether it's over use, as parodied in this skit by Jimmy Fallon & Justin Timberlake (http://leighstjohn.com/hashtag-parody-with-jimmy-fallon-justin-timberlake-late-night-with-jimmy-fallon/) or inappropriate use, there are rules and etiquette for using hashtags.

Here's Twitter's official statement on hashtag use.

"The following behaviors and others like them could cause your account to be filtered from search, or even suspended:

- *Adding one or more topic/hashtag to an unrelated tweet in an attempt to gain attention in search.*

- *Repeatedly tweeting the same topic/hashtag without adding value to the conversation in an attempt to get the topic trending/trending higher.*
- *Tweeting about each trending topic in turn in order to drive traffic to your profile, especially when mixed with advertising.*
- *Listing the trending topics in combination with a request to be followed.*
- *Tweeting about a trending topic and posting a misleading link to something unrelated."*

Another area to be careful when it comes to hashtag use is the actual hashtag itself.

Just like domain names, hashtags suffer from the same problems that arise when any sequence of words is run together without spaces.

When Margaret Thatcher died in April of 2013, one of the hashtags that was used was:

#nowthatchersdead

Now, I don't know about you, but when a lot of people saw that, to them it didn't read "now Thatcher's dead".

Instead it read, "Now that Cher's dead"!

As you can imagine it caused quite a stir – and I would imagine quite a strange day for Cher!

Hashtag 101 by Leigh St John

NOTES:

How do I used hashtags to join a "Twitter Party" or "TweetChat"?

Yes, there is such a thing as a party on Twitter!

TweetChats, also known as Twitter Parties or Twitter Chats, are a wonderful way to engage on Twitter, meet new people, increase your number of followers and engage in interesting conversations with people who share your interests.

Essentially it is a group of users who organize around a specific hashtag at a scheduled time – just like in the physical world when a group of people who want to talk about a certain book at a book club would get together at a scheduled time.

There are a variety of tweetchats going on at any one time and you can find a list by going to: http://tweetreports.com/twitter-chat-schedule/

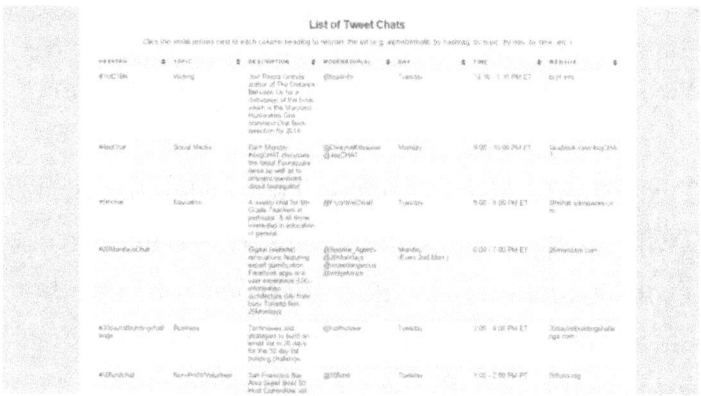

Why on earth would I want to participate in a "tweetchat" you may ask?

First, when you get the hang of it, they can be fun.

Second, you will find that your participation will increase your number of followers and people with whom you are engaging.

Often, just as with a physical book club, these tweetchats happen regularly, as you will see in the previous image.

It can take a little while to get into the swing of how to effective be a part of a tweetchat so don't worry if it's still all a little new at this point.

Just look at some other tweetchats from the list.

By the way, this is another place I like to use TagBoard. If I'm just looking and don't want to participate, I prefer the way they have the posts listed – I find it less distracting.

NOTES:

How do I create my own hashtag?

It doesn't take a fancy program to create a hashtag and apply it to your messages.

Any social media post can include a hashtag, however if you want to create a specific hashtag for your work, your business, your book, your event etc, first you will need to consider what you want to achieve and to come up with something that is short, sharp, straight to the point – and something that other users will be inspired to use in their own posts.

The South by Southwest Interactive, Film and Music Festival occurs every year and the hashtag for the whole event is **#SXSW**. It's short, effective and simple.

The 2015 Super Bowl has a hashtag (among others) of #SB49.

I decided to do a real-world example of this for you and started using the hashtag #inspired2achieve.

For me, everything I am about is helping people not only to achieve their goals, but to be inspired to achieve them. Hence, it worked for me.

Also, I already own the domain name www.inspired2achieve.org, this is where some of my webinars are hosted, and since the .com is only available at a ghastly high price, I figure this is a great place to start.

When I did a search for the hashtag #inspired2achieve I found that only been used about 12 times ever in the entire history of the Internet (and most of those were by me! LOL!), so was a good target for me to start making representative of my own brand.

When you have decided on a hashtag, search Hashtags.org to see if it has already been used or claimed.

Type the hashtag into the Search box in the upper right hand corner of the Hashtags.org page.

When I entered the term #inspired2achieve, it showed no definition.

If there is no definition, that's a good sign. Also, the "Estimated Tweets Per Hour (Based on 1% Sample)" analytics will then tell you how the word is being used. If you don't see a lot of traffic into the hashtag, you may be able to use it without conflict.

Your next step is to define your hashtag by going to https:// hashtags.org/definition/add/. This will set the general parameters of your hashtag's usage.

For example, here is the definition I set for #inspired2achieve:

Next, while you don't need to create a 'tagboard' (www.tagboard.com) I decided I wanted to have a visual representation of the growth of the #inspired2achieve hashtag so this is the one I created:

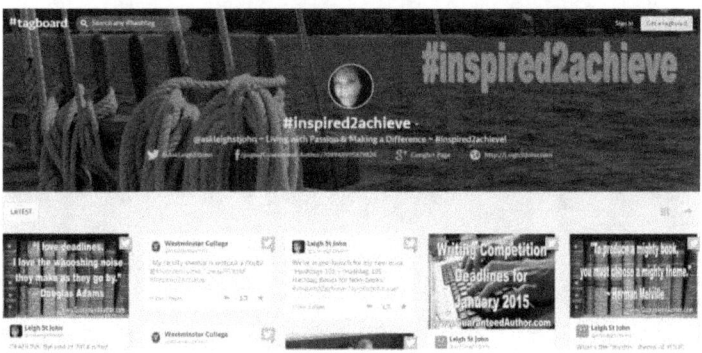

So, at the time of writing this, the hashtag #inspired2achieve is only a couple of weeks old.

As the hashtag you've created develops a following, essentially you are creating a community online.

The biggest thing now is to make sure you are constantly using your hashtag – but only in posts where the content is relevant to your hashtag!

NOTES:

•

Can someone own a hashtag?

While certain terms can be trademarked, and therefore the use of such terms is governed by their trademarks, in general you can't 'own' a hashtag.

Hashtags belong to the community, even if you created it yourself.

You may have created it, given it a definition at hashtags.org, and even registered it at twubs.com (we didn't go into this as registering a hashtag isn't necessary, but feel free to view their website – it's a cool extra step) – but no matter what steps you have taken, unless it is somehow protected under a trademarking law, no one can own a hashtag.

NOTES:

How do I use hashtags to get more followers?

By being persistent with your use of relevant hashtags, you can not only increase the number of followers you have in any social media platform, but you can also increase their level of engagement.

One example of a campaign that did extremely well was #WantAnR8 created for the car brand, Audi. Twitter users would use that hashtag to tell Audi why they would want an R8 for the day, and then whoever submitted the best tweet won a car for the day.

Another way to use hashtags to get more followers is to use trends. We will go into trends in a later chapter, but essentially a trend is a hashtag that is growing in popularity (usage) at a high rate.

By using the trending hashtag in a relevant quote, users who are following that trend who find your post interesting will often click to follow you.

For instance, in Seattle at the moment, one of the trending hashtags on Twitter is #GoHawks (not surprising!)

If you were to post a relevant tweet about the Hawks, every other Hawks fan who is following that hashtag has the possibility of seeing your post and potentially clicking to follow you – if they think you've added something worthwhile.

Does this happen a lot? For a newbie – no. But every single one of us has to start somewhere...

NOTES:

Using Hashtags Offline

While it may seem like hashtags are confined to the realm of the virtual world, they are starting to have an impact in the physical world as well.

In this image, handmade banners with the hashtag #okedrally were being used.

During the 2013 Super Bowl, a staggering 57% of ads featured hashtags!

Bird's Eye foods even released in 2014 a shaped mashed potato food that included forms of @-symbols and hashtags, called "Mashtags".

NOTES:

What are 'trending' hashtags?

A hashtag is considered to be trending when it is either changing rapidly with regard to its popularity, or it is consistently being used be a statistically large number of people and in a statistically large number of posts.

Trends come in three main varieties:
1. Trending up
2. Trending down
3. Constantly popular

If we take a look at hashtags.org, at the time of writing this, here is what is trending on Twitter:

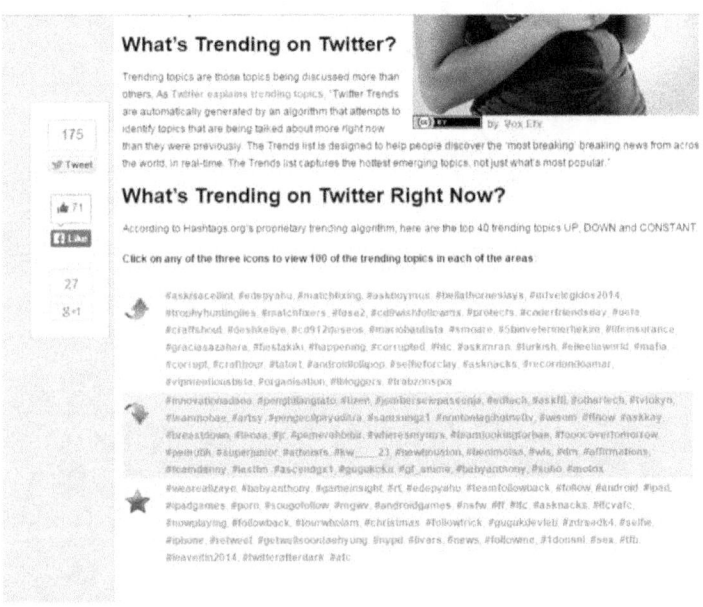

While this may be an interesting list, if we look at it again this time tomorrow, the list may well look decidedly different.

Trends in the online world are not like fashion trends that may stay for a season or even a year or two. In the realm of cyberspace, a topic could be trending today and old news tomorrow.

NOTES:

Hashtags for Writers and Authors

Here are just a few to get you started...

#amwriting

Writing can be an isolating experience, and Twitter is a great way of connecting with other writers – after all, it's us and a keyboard that is usually connected to the Internet, yes? #amwriting is a hashtag started by Johanna Harness as a way of supporting writers and developing a sense of community.

#fridayreads

Friday Reads has become a good way of promoting your books if you can persuade your friends to include you in their #fridayreads! Ideally, include the Twitter @username of the author and if the book has a hashtag use it as well, and a link to where they can buy the book. If you have an Amazon Associates account, you will even earn money if people click the link and buy the book!

And if someone else gives a shoutout to one of your books, make sure that you retweet it on your own Twitter account, and add it to your 'Favorite' tweets.

#bookgiveaway

Running a book giveaway on Twitter?

Use #bookgiveaway to help people discover it.

Here are some more to keep you going...

Connect With Other Writers and Authors

- #AmEditing
- #AmWriting
- #BookMarket
- #IndieAuthors
- #LitChat
- #MemoirChat
- #PoetTues
- #ScriptChat (Screenwriters)
- #WordCount
- #WriteChat
- #WritersLife
- #WriterWednesday
- #WritingParty
- #YALitChat
- #ZineChat

General Writing Information
- o #AskAgent
- o #AskAuthor
- o #AskEditor
- o #BookMarket
- o #BookMarketing
- o #BookMarketing
- o #EBooks
- o #GetPublished
- o #IndiePub
- o #PromoTip
- o #Publishing
- o #PubTip
- o #SelfPub
- o #SelfPublishing
- o #WriteTip
- o #WritingTip

Inspiring Creativity & Productivity
- o #1K1H (write one thousand words in one hour)
- o #Creativity
- o #StoryStarter

- o #WIP (work in progress)
- o #WordAThon
- o #WritingPrompt

Connect With Readers

- o #BookGiveaway
- o #BookGiveaway
- o #FreeBook
- o #FreeDownload
- o #FridayReads
- o #Kindle
- o #LitChat
- o #MustRead
- o #MustRead
- o #Nook
- o #StoryFriday
- o #TeaserTues

Book Marketing

- o #99c (to offer or pick up an eBook bargain)
- o #AuthorRT
- o #BookGiveaway
- o #BookMarketing

- o #FollowFriday
- o #FreebieFriday
- o #FreeReads
- o #Novelines (to quote your own work)

NOTES:

Are hashtags here to stay?

My crystal ball is in at the shop for repairs so I can't give you a definitive answer to that one, however what I can say is that given their prevalence and popularity – and the manner in which they are being used to support people's online activity and engagement, I don't see them going anywhere.

Although some don't yet understand them, and others feel they are somehow above using them, the simple fact is that if you want to truly engage in a meaningful way in the world of social media, you need to embrace hashtags.

About the Author

www.LeighStJohn.com

When you meet Leigh St John you understand the meaning of the word "passion" – she lives & breathes it with an enthusiasm that is contagious!

Leigh's writing credits are too numerous to list and include authoring several published non-fiction books, ghost-writing over twenty books and several successful blogs, being an Expert Columnist with one of the leading small business magazines, Editor of her own publication, and literally hundreds of published articles.

One of Leigh's greatest passions is helping Writers achieve their dream of becoming Published Authors!

While I may now have the majority of the answers to successfully writing and self-publishing, it hasn't always been this way...

For years I was like you probably are right now... with one or more books inside you, longing to come out... but they never did...

I know what it feels like to tell friends "I'm going to finish my book this year and finally get it published," only to have that statement haunt you months, years later when the book is still un-finished and un-published...

...but one day I reached a point where I said "enough" and I made a commitment to write, to be published and to stop letting excuses get in the way of achieving my dreams!

That day was made waaaaaay back in 1990 and since then I've achieved more than I ever dreamed... including having an *Amazon #1 Best-Seller*!

Here's what my professional bio looks like today – when you read it, think of all the ways my Team and I can help support you to achieve YOUR dreams...

Leigh is an **Achievement Strategist** - a published Author, Media Personality & MC, Speaker, Facilitator, Strategic Consultant, Coach & Trainer who, quite simply, makes things happen!

Whether it's coaching clients to become published authors, helping you to effectively brand yourself (personal and/or business) in order to exponentially grow your business, facilitating joint ventures, developing and rolling out strategic and marketing plans with clients, or consulting in any one of a variety of areas, Leigh specializes in getting the client from A to Z in the most effective - profitable and enjoyable! – manner.

With her unique background in commercial & non-profit management, web design and social media, education, entertainment and media, a Client List that reads like a who's who, & her passion for making a positive difference in the world, Leigh St John brings with her an exciting blend of experience & understanding that generates results!

Leigh is a member of Mensa, Executive Director of The Masters Media Group (encompassing Senior Guide USA and various online state Senior Guides), & an accomplished entrepreneur in her own right (having created both wonderfully successful businesses & a couple of memorable failures – though thankfully more of the former than the latter).

Her media and presentation background includes hosting movies premieres at Warner Bros to black-tie charity events through to week-long corporate professional development retreats. She has coached international trade delegations on behalf of the Australian government and much more.

Leigh has taught for many years with one of the world's top business schools (despite not having finished high school!), has qualifications in Journalism, Non-Profit Management & Adult Education... Leigh has studied Psychology, Marketing & Communications...

...and she studied Artificial Intelligence at Stanford University for a semester – for fun!

Leigh is also a member of the Council on Foundations & is licensed with the Commission for Children & Young People [License # 7849/78846].

Other Books authored by Leigh **include:**
- "Achievement Alchemist"
- "365 Days of Inspiration"
- "What Do I Want To Be?"
- "Escaping the Small Business Syndrome"
- "Non-Profit Profitability"

Projects and Activities (Past and Present) also include:

- Executive Director, Masters Media Group (includes Nevada Senior Guide & Senior Guide USA)
- Owner and Coach, Guaranteed Author Program ~ www.GuaranteedAuthor.com
- Owner, 'Writing and Publishing My Book'
- Web Producer for the Emmy-Nominated, "Trafficked No More" documentary
- Founding Board Member, Crowdfunding Professional Association
- Board Member, "Courtroom Cuddlies" (Non-Profit Organization providing 'fluffy friends' to children in courtroom situations)
- Host – "Going Green TV"
- Host – "Quiet Achievers and Unsung Heroes" radio talk show
- Executive Director, Senior Industry Network Group
- Relationship Manager - Conference Online Las Vegas
- Associate Director – Corps of Compassion/Caring 4 Kids Foundation (501c3 Non-Profit Organization)
- Consulting Lecturer and Facilitator for Mt Eliza Centre for Executive Education (listed by Forbes Magazine as one of the world's top business schools)
- Member of AFI (American Film Institute)

- Ambassador for the Social Register of Las Vegas
- Member of Mensa
- Founder of the Australian Mentoring Institute Inc (Non-Profit Organization)
- Board Member and Community Outreach Chair, NAWBO (National Association of Women Business Owners)
- Member of the Panel of Professional Advisers for the Victorian Government
- Founding Member of the Women In Tourism International Alliance (WITIA)
- Australian Ambassador to the International Virtual Women's Chamber of Commerce
- Mensa National Special Interest Coordinator
- Speaker Chair, Las Vegas Shared Vision Network
- Finalist in the Australian Women in Business Awards
- Finalist in the Telstra Business Woman of the Year Awards
- Expert Columnist, "Dynamic Small Business Magazine", Australia's leading small business magazine
- Daily Columnist – "The Morning Bulletin – Life With Leigh" (full page every weekday covering 'positive' news stories in major metropolitan newspaper)
- Drive-Time Co-Host, major commercial radio station

- Sponsor and Mentor for Australian Business Week (business simulation program for high school students)
- Mentor for the Commonwealth New Enterprise Incentive Scheme Advisory Committee – NEISAC – (government-sponsored small business start-up project)
- Judge – Australian Film Institute Awards
- Judge – SIFE (Students in Free Enterprise) National Awards
- Judge – APICTA (Asia Pacific Information Communications and Telecommunications Awards)

On the personal side, my passions include (not in any particular order) ...

Good red wine, my glorious friends, the joy I feel from helping people achieve their dreams, my beloved classic convertible Jaguar I'm restoring little by little (her name is Baby), waking up to see rainbows on my wall brought to life by the crystal candle holder on the windowsill, road trips, living in the USA, Italian food, books, being on or near the water... and generally being 'happy'...

At my core, I loves to smile and to make others smile - and get a thrill beyond words when I can truly help someone to see their own potential and increase their confidence.

I have faith in the power of the human spirit and that we each have the ability to achieve whatever we believe in and anything upon which we focus our intention and inspired actions!

I believe Faith, Gratitude, Allowing and Love are among the most powerful forces in the Universe.

My go-to Scripture when I need that extra dose of 'something':

"Commit thy way unto the Lord; trust in Him, and He shall bring it to pass." Psalm 37:5

Someone once asked me what I would like to have people think of me after I have left this dimension and moved on to the next. I have since thought about that question and my answer is this:

"I hope that I have made people smile and that in some small way I have helped them to realize that they have unlimited potential; and assisted and inspired them to increase their confidence, believe in the power of their dreams, and discover the strategies they need to realize those dreams. With faith, focus and determined, inspired action, anything truly is possible!"

"All our dreams can come true – if we have the courage to pursue them." – Walt Disney

For more information:
www.LeighStJohn.com